THE INK
OF ME

By: Michelle Brown

Publisher

The Inner Child of Me
@2022 by Michelle Brown

Printed in USA

SPECIAL THANKS

First, I want to give thanks to my Lord and Savior, Jesus Christ, for giving me the vision to author this book. Special thanks to mom for always being my biggest supporter, always teaching me right from wrong, and encouraging me to always keep going. This woman is so strong in many ways. I love her to the moon and back. Thanks to all my siblings for being there with me throughout everything, and all my friends who have been on this long rollercoaster ride with me. I especially want to give thanks to Author Cornelious Woody Sr. for your guidance and help along the way.

Table of Contents

CHAPTER 1- UNBORN

{ABUSE}

My name is Chelle. I was born April 28, 1992, to John Adams and Quanny Lee on the east side of Detroit. My parents had a beautiful relationship. They did everything together, movies, skating, picnics, etc.

They were extremely close like best friends. Most people were jealous of the relationship and wanted to be just like them. Some even called them Bonny & Clyde. The relationship was so beautiful that they were on the road to being married. My parents were the couple every child and adult would want to see. Their relationship topped all couples. My dad, John Adams, was truly a big gentleman towards my mom, Quanny Lee. He worshipped the ground she walked on.

He tried to hide it from my mom, she knew something was not right. His behavior started to change, and he became very controlling towards my mom. He did not want to tell anyone, but he had to reveal it to my mom because in their relationship they did not hide anything.

They told each other everything. They always kept it 100 percent no matter how hard the truth was to tell. They simply didn't keep anything secretive. So, when my mom asked, he had no choice but to tell her the at the time my mother was working for Burger King and Taco Bell. My dad was also working. He was junking, picking up metal and stuff people would throw out as trash, and scrap for money. He also had a part-time job at Dominos. So, both of my parents always worked and kept a job. They were not only perfect in the relationship, but they brought everything together. However, even with all the rainbows and stars, my mom would soon start to experience a major storm.

My dad started using drugs. Although truth. She knew he was using drugs when she got him the job at the hotel working with my great auntie.

My dad was out there bad. Often, mom would have to get him out of dope houses or buy his I.D. back from the dope man. My dad sold and did anything to get a fix. And if he didn't get it, then someone would have to pay for it. He would cause major hell stealing, lying, and just doing anything to get his drugs. He was really playing in the devils' playground. Drugs were literally being allowed to take over his entire body.

Then he started beating my mom. While she was pregnant with my sibling, he punched her in the stomach until she had a miscarriage. So yes, there was a baby before me. Sadly, my mom lost it due to my dad's abuse. After the loss of my sibling, she would soon become pregnant again with me. This still didn't stop the abuse. If you were to ask mom, she will say it got even worse. Several times, he even tried to kill her. The lady he once loved and cared for he started to treat her like a punching bag.

My mom could not believe the man who was her best friend and lover would become one of her worst nightmares. "I'm sorry," followed by, "I'll never do it again." would come after each beating. My mom kept forgiving him thinking he would change.

She had never experienced this type of abuse before, except something a little bit similar with my Grandma Cindy's boyfriend. This man would beat and torture both my grandma and mom. He was also on drugs. His name was Jake. He the worst man besides my dad that my mom encountered. He abused my mom, and my grandma. Jake would rape my mom. This pattern continued from the age of seven to ten years old.

One time Jake beat my Granny Cindy because she wanted to go to church. "Jake was so angry that he pulled all my granny's hair out." All he could not pull out, he cut off. He would also play Russian roulette with both my grandma and mom. So, when mom met my dad, he just added to the abuse.

So many thoughts went through mom's mind. Sometimes she thought she deserved the abuse. Or maybe if he didn't do drugs, he would not beat her. And especially, how could someone she loved so much and loved her try to destroy and kill her?

He not only abused my mom, but when she was pregnant with me, he pushed her down a flight of stairs. My mom knew for sure she was going to lose me, but the greater power up above, Our Father, shielded both of us. Still, she kept going back to my dad. However, they never stayed together under the same roof with all the beating he put on her. She was terrified to get a house with an abusive man. Moving in with him would be insane to her. So, she would just spend nights at my granny's and aunt's houses. He would spend nights with my mom at her great granny's house.

The abuse continued throughout my mom's pregnancy with me. When she was five months pregnant with me, "she went to take bath." My dad locked her in the room. Then he poured gasoline on mom and set her on fire. Fortunately, it would not stay lit in the bathtub. That still didn't stop his desire to kill my mom.

My dad was very controlling. One day, mom's cousins, Kim and Linda, "brought friends over." Dad thought mom was lying to him, and one of the guys was for her. This wasn't true, but you couldn't convince dad it wasn't. So, he went into the bathroom while my mom was trying to take a bath. With the curlers plugged up he threw them in the tub with my mom and beat her. She still stayed with him.

Although he was very controlling, he could not control mom like he wanted. This was one of the reasons why my mom got beat. There were multiple times his abusive ways would harm her. He even put her in the hospital before.

Finally, mom got the courage to leave him. She was so petrified. He had beat her up so much. My mom had to leave because she had my older sister, Nicky, at the time. She was only one year old, and mom was still pregnant with me. She didn't want us to grow up thinking it was okay for men to beat on women. or to stay with a guy that was beating us.

Unfortunately, the apple didn't fall too far from the tree for my dad. My dad's mom, which was my Granny Anita's kids' father, beat her also. One time, dad witnessed his mom and dad fight. His dad choked his mom. But my granny Anita was tired of it, so she put up a fight by grabbing a lamp and hitting him in the face while my aunt picked up a chair and hit him right across his back.

At the age of 17, dad and his friend were sitting at a table drinking. After they left the house, four guys jumped on my dad and hit him in the head with a two by four. With bloody knuckles and muddy clothes, they left him there in the snow for dead. Two elderly people saw my dad and called the police. Also, around this time, they told my granny, and took him to the hospital. He was in a coma for two weeks.

The doctors told my granny that half of his brain was not functioning and not to upset him or make him mad. Dad had to learn how to walk and talk again. My granny was the one who had to teach my 17-year-old dad how to walk and talk. She had to take baby steps with him. My dad was a fighter. Even with his traumatic situation, he still fought through it. People would always come and get him when they got into altercations so he could fight their battles for them.

My dad was very protective of his loved ones. One time, my Aunt Tiny got shot because of a jealous ex-boyfriend. He knew she had another man but wanted to get back with her. My aunt didn't want the same. This ex-boyfriend came to her house and kicked the door in, but she managed to run out the back door. He then got in his car and chased her. Once he got close enough, he shot her in the neck, and fled back to his house. When my dad found out about it, he was seething. No one could stop him. My dad went looking for my aunt's ex-boyfriend. He went to his house and asked his mom where he was. With tears in her eyes, she told him he had shot himself and was dead. My dad replied, "Good, because I came to kill him myself."

The injury to the head triggered my dad when he became angry. So, when my mom met my dad, his anger had died down until he started using drugs. When the drugs got in his system, it not only triggered him, but also the brain that was not functioning at full capacity due to the trauma. The doctors told my Granny Anita that my dad was not to drink or take any type of drugs because it would trigger his anger. They also cautioned that he would not be able to control his anger either. So, no one was to make anger in no type of way.

Around the time of my mom leaving, she started attending a church. There she got baptized and she spoke in tongues, all the time still pregnant with me. Our Heavenly Father had protected us by his angels the whole time we were in the fire!

CHAPTER 2- NEWBORN

{THE MADNESS CONTINUES}

Even after mom mustered up the courage to finally leave my abusive dad, it still didn't stop him from continuing to attack us. "One day at my great grandmother's house" weeks after being hit by a drunk driver, mom was trying to stop my brother's uncle baby's mother from getting hit because she was pregnant. My mom didn't even know she was pregnant with my brother, Terry, at the time. His uncle's baby's mother went under the car and my mom busted the windshield. He threw my mom on the other side of the street and then pulled over and went back in the store to get something else to drink - right after hitting my mom. So, all my mom's guy friends beat him up.

My mom literally died that day. All she could remember was going into a black hole. There, she called on the Lord. She didn't even know she was pregnant. She just knew she had a one-year-old and a three-month-old baby. She said, "Lord who going to take care of my kids?" And the Lord shot her back down to Earth. There she was lying in the street when a white Chevy tried to take her head off. Good thing, my brother's cousin, Evete, grabbed her and conveyed her to the sidewalk.

My mother couldn't walk or talk. Her mouth was split open from the accident. About a couple weeks after this tragedy, my dad found a way to get back in touch with my mom. So, since she didn't want to be with my dad. "He got on the phone and told her that he was going to mess her up worst." My Aunt Kim grabbed the phone and said, "You dumb motherfucker she can't even walk, and you threatening her?" He was like, "Fuck that Bitch and you too!" He went on to say, "I am going break her legs, and when I get there, I am messing you up Kim." "So, my mother and aunt made up their minds," when he came, they were going to get him beat up.

It was a party that night for my mom's cousin's son. My dad always carried out what he said. When he got there, they let my Aunt Kim's cousin and uncle beat my dad up. Being bruised up and getting thrown into a table didn't stop my dad's anger. He went and hid.

Everybody thought he had left, but he hid in the closet. They called the police, but when they arrived, the police felt bad for my dad, and let him go. After they let him go, he came back to my grandmother's house, firebombed it. With my aunt Kim asleep and me laying in her bed, my dad set the whole room on fire. My mom and brother Terry's uncle were in the kitchen when my aunt Kim told my mom, "There was something, I was supposed to tell you." My mom thought, okay girl love you too. When they got to the door, she opened it and said, "I know what I was supposed to tell you. My room is on fire." Then they grabbed me out the bed. My father above protected me from that fire. Not only that time at around six months old, but more memories ahead that proved His angels always had me.

CHAPTER 3- AGE 1-3

{WHEN TRAGEDY HAPPENS}

My mom always loved nursing. It's her passion. While attending Ross Medical School she paid my great aunt to babysit us. Mom would soon find out that my great aunt's son, Timothy, was touching my sister, Nicky. Nicky told mom when he gave her baths, he would touch her.

At the time, Timothy was about 11 years old, and my sister had to be two, going on three years old. When mom found out, she and her friend took us to Children's hospital to be checked out. I was 1 years old, but he had not touched me. It was just my sister, Nicky.

My grandma and everybody else, raised them because they didn't want to see them on the streets. My mom practically raised him and his siblings. She's the one who taught his sister how to walk. "They parents was out they lives" for a long time in their younger years and half their older lives. So, this hurt mom at the inner most core.

Later that week, my mom let my dad keep me because my auntie used to ask if she could see me. My mom did. One day he called mom and "told her if she didn't come to get me, he was going to throw me off the Belle Isle Bridge." So, while she was walking up Gratiot on her way to my brother's dad's house to get some help, he pulled up on my mom. He had left me with my aunt. Since my mom didn't want to be with him anymore, he kidnapped her, raped her, and then tried to kill her. He beat her for hours. My mom thought she was dead, but once again God spared her life and protected her.

I was still one year old at the time. My mom ended up getting pregnant. So, she would have had my sister, me, and my little brother, Terry, plus the baby if she had kept it, but she didn't. She got an abortion.

Later she met her husband, and my stepdad, King Sr., on the bus. They got married and had four kids, King jr., Kathy, Kaleb, Kase, his biological kids. He also raised me, my sister, and my brother. Mom still allowed my dad to see me, although he had been abusive in the past.

One day when I was two something happened, and I didn't know that would be the last time seeing him. While my stepdad was at school, my dad came over to see me. He ended up trying to fight my mom and trying to force her to have sex with him. That's when my mom made up in her mind that he couldn't see me anymore until I was old enough to see him on my own!

At two years old, I also battled with seizures. This happened until I turned three. My seizures got so bad I almost died. My mom had never seen me like this before because I would always come back from them. But not this time. It got so bad I was hospitalized.

My mom and stepdad rushed me to St. John's hospital. Doctors kept saying it was my mom's fault and that she beat me to the point of having a seizure. They accused her of a lot, especially in an attempt to explain why I wasn't responding. Eventually, they told my parents they needed to take me to Children's Hospital because there wasn't anything they could do to help. Plus, they wanted money. Thankfully, my stepdad was like, "No, my baby staying here!" He offered to pay them 4,000 dollars just to keep me in the hospital. He was going off on all the nurses and doctors because they were still trying to put me out of the hospital.

My mom and great grandmother were firm believers that if you call on His name, Jesus, and trust in His word, you were healed. So, they both began to lay hands upon me and pray. Prayer changes things because 20 years later I have not had one seizure or symptom of it.

CHAPTER 4- AGES 5-9
{SICK IN THE HEAD}

"It was tough for my mother to raise seven children, but together her and my stepdad made it work." They ended up buying a house at 186 East Grixdale in Detroit, Michigan. I'll never forget this house or address. My mom and her husband, having the heart they had, allowed my great aunt's children to come and stay with them. Since Timothy and his siblings were in high school and mom wanted them to graduate, she offered them a place to stay at our house.

My mom was working at the time and her husband was a big drug dealer, so they were gone most of the time. "My siblings and I were too young to watch ourselves." Since my cousins were there, they started watching us. "But my cousin, Timothy, was not just watching us, he was also molesting me." He would have these nude magazines and his sick mind would have a six-year-old demonstrate some of this stuff. I cannot really remember all the stuff he would have me do. I just know it was nasty and I can remember Vaseline was involved. He would touch me and have me touching and sucking on his penis. At the time I didn't understand what was going on "I was too young to know what I was doing," but I know it influenced me and my sisters.

For Nicky it was both brothers and they would bend her over. I do not know if it was both touching me. What they would do is tell us we could have some caramel candy apples and fruit snacks. They were truly sick in the head. We were in elementary school, attending Greenfield Park at the time. They were in high school. They have no excuse for taking our innocence. Later we found out they was not just touching me and my sister, Nicky, "They were also touching my lil sister Kathy." So, they were beyond sick in the head.

How could you damage someone's childhood like that? This caused a lot of traumas for me, and especially my sisters. I remember attending Hutchinson Elementary school and my sister, Nicky, would allow boys to hit her on the butt and they would call each other mommy and daddy.

The funny part is I was never a fighter in school, but my sister would always get me and tell me the little boys kept hitting her on the butt on the playground. When recess came around, little ole me found the little boys and told them "If you hit my sister on the butt one more time, it's going to be on." They wouldn't do it again on that day, but eventually did it again on another day. I chased them until we got stopped by one of the teachers and I told them what had happened.

Of course, the little boys got in trouble. I teased them and said, "That's what you get. Should have just listened."

{EMBARRASSED}

During that same time, it was hard for me to focus on school. I was failing all my classes. I can remember one day in class. "I had to be about five years old when I was taking a spelling test." I always cheated. I would lean over to see what my classmates put down as answers. When report cards came out my grades were terrible. I had all "F's." My sister Nicky was always smart.

I do not know why I listened to her, but while we were riding the bus home, she asked to see my report card. She showed all the kids on the bus my report card. I was so embarrassed that when I got home, I told my mom. Nicky got in trouble for doing that to me. That was not the only thing she did to me.

On one of my birthdays, she had me pass out all my money to the kids at school. My sister

Nicky was irritating for doing that. However, she was older than me. I guess that's why I listened to her.

{ACTING OUT}

Being molested caused Nicky and I to act out sexually. Being exposed to sexual things at an early age damaged us. We would playhouse often. One time my mom caught us under the bed with her best friend's nephew. Also, at nine years old I had my first puppy love, as some would call it.

We dated brothers that stayed next door to us. The window in our room was right across from where their window was. So, while we were in the room my sister and I were dancing in the window and listening to Brandy's song, "Have You Ever" on tape. We started stripping and taking off our clothes. My sister Nicky and I were in our panties putting on a real show for them, at least we thought we were.

My parents never knew because we never said anything about taking off our clothes. But we did tell them our cousins were molesting us while they were not at home. Eventually we would find out years later that it was multiple victims in the family who had endured the same thing.

This was the house where it all started and began. 186 E. Grixdale

CHAPTER 5- AGES 11-15

{JACKSON TOWN}

While still attending Greenfield Park Elementary school, we were living on 6 mile. I was in the fifth grade when my mom and stepdad started having problems. My sister Nicky had told the counselor at our school that he was touching on our lil sister, Kase. She didn't say our cousins. She accused our stepdad. This caused child protective services to get involved.

One day they came down to our school. One by one we were called into a room and was asked if we had been touched by our dad. I said no because he had never touched me sexually. My sister Nicky later told them that she lied. She almost caused me and all my siblings to be taken away. While we were under investigation, they would come to the house. He wasn't allowed to be in the house or around us. This was also one of the reasons my mom left and moved to Jackson, Michigan.

I was 11 years old when all my siblings and mom lived in a shelter called Interfaith. This shelter treated us so good. We had three meals a day plus a snack at night. They would also provide us with clothes and shoes.

We stayed for a few months, so my mom signed us up for Frost Elementary School. We would catch the bus from the shelter to the school. It offered a lot of stuff my school back in Detroit, Michigan didn't offer. They had music class, and the lunch food was good also. I was the teacher's helper so I would pass out soap and paper towel during bathroom breaks and pass out paper and pencils in class.

The shelter was good. It had a playground for the kids who were living there but it still didn't stop the boredom. With seven children, my mom wanted to find us stuff to do so she asked the people in the shelter if there were any parks or centers around where she could take us. They told her there was a park up the street which was attached to a school. My mom gathered all seven of us up and we went walking to the park. At the park, my three sisters and I stayed on the side my mom was at, and my three brothers went to the basketball court. There me and my sister, Nicky, met boyfriends. They were brothers.

At the time I didn't talk to the brother, Paul. I liked him, but I never was the type to approach a boy, even if I liked him. So, my sister started talking to the other brother, Carl. The brother, Paul, started talking to our friend, Sally. One of the little brothers would call her salad. My sister and her boyfriend, Carl, played like they got married at the park. He gave her a ring; Paul gave Sally a necklace.

Nicky lost the ring when my mom was house looking. We went into this one house that had fleas and bugs. They got all over us and my sister shook so badly she shook the ring right off. When we got back to the shelter, we all hopped in the shower. She told her boyfriend, Carl, what had happened. He told her, "It's okay. I will get you another one." After that we had went to Sally's aunt's house. My sister, Nicky, was on the phone talking to the brothers. Paul got on the phone and told my sister, "I do not want talk to Sally anymore. I want to talk to Chelle." Sally heard it and she threw her necklace across the room. I was smiling because I liked him too and didn't understand why he wanted to talk to Sally in the first place. I should've felt bad, but I really didn't because I was too busy thinking, I got my man....

We started talking and the four of us were inseparable. We always were together.

They would come down to the shelter to visit us and we would go to the park and play. One time, we even went to their house when they lived on First Street. We met their grandma, mom and other siblings. My mom liked them too, so she called them her sons. They were gentlemen. They treated me and Nicky with respect, so whenever we did something, my mom would ask Carl and Paul if they wanted to come. The time we were going to the movies to see *Freddy vs. Jason*, they were supposed to attend with us, but couldn't because they got grounded for sneaking out of the house to see *King Kong*. We ended up leaving because my mom friend got into some trouble. Plus, my mom was going back to her husband, King Sr. We didn't get a chance to tell Paul and Carl we were leaving. It happened suddenly.

CHAPTER 6- AGE 12

{FIRST KISS}

I was 12 years old attending A.L. Holmes Elementary/Middle School when I saw my dad again. My mom was working as a sub, lunch aid, and school officer. I don't know how she contacted him, but she called me in the office one day and was like, "Do you want to talk to your daddy?" I was thinking she was talking about my current daddy. All I knew was her husband King Sr. So, I was confused when she said, John. I hunched my shoulders as if I didn't care to talk to him.

After the conversation, my mom decided we were going to see him. He was living on this street called Dexter. "He had a small little studio." When we came over my mom and him talked while I just swung in a chair acting nonchalant because my attitude was, "I don't know you and didn't want to." I only went because of my mom. "They continued talking and eventually my mom, me, and all my siblings moved in his studio for couple days until my mom left to go back to the Interfaith Shelter in Jackson, MI.

I was still 12 years old when we got there. My sister Nicky and I kept wondering about what if we ran back into Carl and Paul while back in Jackson, MI. Somehow Carl got the notice that we were back, so he came up there to see us. When we saw him, we were shocked because he was short and fat the last time, we saw him. Now he was tall and slim. He ended up telling his brother Paul. The next day Paul came back to the shelter with Carl.

We were having dinner. People had to stand in line and "the outsiders ate after they fed the residents." So, me and Paul went outside. He asked, "You want to get back together?" Really, we never broke up, my family just left. Then he lifted my chin up and gave me my first kiss. After that it was back to normal, Chelle and Paul, and Carl and Nicky. You couldn't tell us anything. We would sit outside the shelter doors and hug each other. They were both taller than me and my sister, Nicky. So, Nicky would have to get picked up, and "I would have to step on Paul's toes to lift myself up to kiss."

My mom would give us her bridge card and we would go down to Frank's Liquor Store on the corner and buy snacks. We'd sit in front of the shelter till it got dark and they had gone home. Then we had to get ready for bed.

One of my best Christmases was at the shelter. From December 20th, all the way to Christmas day we were receiving gifts. Not just any kind of gift. We were getting good gifts! I had a manikin doll head. My siblings had cars, teddy bears, and other gifts. The people who gave us the gifts also came and sang Christmas carols to us. We also took pictures. The shelter even gave us a Christmas party. Together my siblings and I had big black garbage bags full of toys, and gifts.

My dad came down around this time. He stayed on the men's side, and he didn't like it. Neither did he like the fact that I had a boyfriend, so he ended up convincing my mom to move back with him. So, the next day my sister and I had to tell our boyfriends, Carl and Paul, that we were leaving. We then went back to our room to find something we could give them before we left. I gave Paul a bear and a picture of me. My sister gave Carl a teddy bear and a picture of herself also.

Paul gave me a Chicago Bulls jersey and a shirt he had hand drawn himself of *BeBe Kids* with his name at the bottom of it. I kept that shirt up to the day I went back to college. I thought, 'I'm never going see this person again.' I would wear the shirt as a nightgown. It was so big! Carl gave my sister a jersey and a belt with his name on it.

When we moved back with my dad, my sister, Nicky, would sneak to talk to Carl. She would get money to talk on the payphone. I was right along with her. We got caught and my dad was mad like, "What the fuck is a Carl and Paul??!!" He had the belt Carl had given Nicky. He told us we couldn't talk to them anymore. That still didn't stop Nicky though. She found ways to contact them.

CHAPTER 7- AGE 13

{HEARTBREAK}

Winterhalter Elementary/Middle School is where I got my first suspension because I came to class late. My classroom was hidden behind a wall and the school was a little big. It was hard to remember where my classroom was so by the time I found my class, I was late. I had to give my teacher pushups, but I refused. So, she sent me to the office. They asked me for my parents' phone numbers. I didn't know because we had just moved so they sent me back to class. My teacher asked me again to give her ten pushups. I gave up and decided to do them. However, when I did them my teacher and classmates said I was doing the snake. She suspended me and told me I could only come back if my parents came, and I admitted to doing the snake.

I went home and told my mom and dad what had happened. They weren't too happy, so they took me back to school the next day.

My teacher talked to them and asked me, "Now wasn't you doing the snake?"

I told her, "Again, no I was doing the pushups you asked me to do." I had to do my three-day suspension because I would not admit to doing the snake.

We stayed with my dad for a couple of months until my mom got back in touch with her husband, King Sr. He told her he was sick and couldn't walk. He had a cane when we saw him. My mom eventually went back. We stayed in a hotel for a couple days. I was 13 years old when my mom broke it down to me that I wasn't allowed to talk or see my dad till I got older too. It was going to bring conflict between King Sr and my mom. So, it would be best if I didn't have any contact with my dad.

I didn't understand, so it really made me feel confused. Like how did she expect me to just act like he didn't exist? Although I knew she was trying to avoid confrontation with her husband because he had been in my life all this time helping her take care of me, it still hurt. I remember the day we left I cried like a newborn baby. My nose was running. I was full of tears. In the beginning, I felt like I was doing fine and not caring about anything. I wasn't even calling him dad. His name for me was Mr. John until I heard my siblings calling him dad. I was like that's *my* daddy, so I started calling him dad too.

He showed me little things. Like when we walked, he said a man supposed to be walking on the side of the street where cars are coming so if anything happens, they could push you to the side and they'll take whatever is coming. That really stuck with me as well as just his presence overall. Although I did get a whooping once which felt more like a beating to me.

When we were living with him one of my siblings touched his magazine. He was very mad and upset about it. My brother, Terry, and I were being silly. I laughed about everything. I'm very silly, which caused me to get in trouble so many times. Anyways, my dad was like, "what's funny? You think this funny?" He got an extension cord, and I got a whooping for it. That still didn't stop the way I felt for my dad for a second. I was very heartbroken when I had to stop talking to him.

{I CAN SHOW YOU BETTER THAN I CAN TELL YOU}

My brother, Terry, wasn't that much younger than me. We were 11 months apart. He always got me in trouble and that wasn't the only time with my dad. When we were attending A.L. Holmes Elementary/ Middle School, some of my siblings attended tutoring after school together. My brother Terry and I had gotten brand new outfits, so we wanted to show off our clothes to our friends at school. My mom warned, "Don't go up there." All we heard was her music banging. My stepdad always had sounds, even in my mom's car. So, we all like aye, then she hit the corner with a hard turn. I knew we were in trouble.

She got out of the car with switches. I got it, but my brother kept running around the car, so he didn't get hit. That wasn't the end of it. Once home, my mom got some more switches, and I got whipped in front of the neighbors. My mom wanted to make sure I remembered that whooping, and I did. Even to this day, some of my friends still talk about it. They say, "Chelle, remember that time when you got a whooping in front of the school?" Yes, that day is going down in history.

My mom didn't play. If she told you to do something and you didn't, you better believe there was a punishment behind it. I was raised on the old school teachings. My mom didn't care about no child protective services, she would say "call them and I'm a still be whooping you when they get here. You either going to listen to me or you going to get your ass beat. No child I birth in this world will disrespect or feel like they can do what they want to in my house. I brought you in this world and I'll take you out."

My brother Terry was going to leave. My mom told him, "You can leave, but not with my clothes on. You came with nothing. You leave with nothing." My mom really lived by that, and she made sure all of us knew what she was talking about. I can remember plenty of times my siblings got in trouble because they thought my mom was playing. My mom also didn't play when it came to school. She always told us, "Education is the key and you either going to graduate from Quanny house or you going to graduate from the pin house." My mom was something else. She never sugar coated anything with us. So, if my siblings messed up in school they got in trouble. My sister, Nicky, got slapped before in class because she was disrespecting the teacher. My brother King Jr. Got in trouble at school while he was in class. The teacher called my mom and told mom to give him some encouraging words. My mom was like, "You better sit your motherfucking ass down before I break your motherfucking neck."

I'm like, "Dang mom, you had to say it like that?"

She was like, "I bet he sat down."

My mom would always pop up at our school. So, when my friends would say skip with them, I'm like, "Naw, my mom always popping up. You never know when she is coming, so I pass." I was too afraid to skip, and she came up to the school and I wasn't there. I think I would have had to write a whole chapter about how bad I got a whooping for skipping school. My mom would come up to the school with belts around her neck ready to whoop on somebody. She always went to our parent teacher conferences. I had perfect attendance in school. My mom didn't believe in missing school. She told us if your body parts are not falling off you going to school sick in all. She'd bring the medicine to school if got that bad.

One time my brother Terry went to school with mixed match shoes. He was being funny because he was always the class clown. All the teachers and staff knew him because he stays in trouble. I loved my mom. As a child I didn't understand her discipline, but now I do.

{FRESHMAN YEAR}

Everything was going good with my mom and her husband, but he was a big drug dealer. He used to cheat on my mom behind her back, but it was never in her face. He kept it a secret. But my mom knew he was cheating, so it caused problems in the relationship. Plus, he was controlling so my mom would leave to get away from him.

She once left and moved to Anderson, Indiana. I attended one of their middle schools and graduated from there. My siblings and I met some awesome people there. My sister, Nicky, and I became volunteers at this kid's program. We would go on trips and do activities. Often, we were broken up into groups by ages and would be assigned to a group. That part was fun but because we didn't have a car and we were in the country part it was boring. I wanted to go back to Detroit, Michigan. Once again, my mom talked to her husband, and we moved back.

I was soon to start high school. I was attending Henry Ford High School for the 9th grade. I can remember my mom saying, "Chelle, they gone get you," because there was a lot of females that were lesbians at the time. I didn't let that stop me though. I still went. My sister, Nicky, was in the 10th grade. I was 15 years old because I failed first grade and it put me a grade behind. I will never forget my freshman year. It was so lit.

We had fire drills every Friday because some students would set lockers on fire. We would have fights all the time. One time there was a shootout in the hallway. So, the school was on lockdown. I remember one of the boys at the school set this teacher's hair on fire because he didn't like her. It got so bad my mom was trying to take Nicky and I out of the school.

She tried to put us in Southwestern because the principal was about her business. When we got to the school, the principal didn't waste any time. She laid down the rules and what wasn't allowed. She made students go home if they didn't have the right shirt on. My mom was like, "Yes! I like her!" My sister and I looked at each other and was like, "No!" Good thing we didn't attend the school though. We stayed at Henry Ford.

The most dangerous, but exciting time for me was the day our principal was leaving the school. The students went crazy. We had a riot. They were jumping on teachers' cars. Some were destroying them by throwing bricks at the cars, and busting teachers' windows out. The police were there macing kids and sending them to jail if they didn't cooperate. We even had helicopters! It was so entertaining, and I wanted to watch everything.

My sister, Nicky, was like, "Let's go home."

But I was like, "I want to stay."

She was like, "They are taking motherfuckers to jail!"

They had blocked down the streets, so we had to go straight up seven mile. With me just starting high school that was exciting to me because I didn't see any action like that in middle school.

While we were still attending Henry Ford High School, I can remember the time Nicky was to be in a play called *The Wiz*. When she was rehearsing, I stayed after school with her. One day we got hungry. There was a gas station and a few restaurants close by the school, so we decided to go to the gas station and get some snacks. On our way back to school, a car ran the red light and hit my siter, Nicky. I was so shocked. I couldn't believe what had just happened. I heard voices, and people screaming, "Did you get the license plate? Did you see the driver?" However, I was so stunned that I blanked out.

The interesting part was I always told my sibling, "If I ever see you get hit by a car, I will laugh." But I didn't laugh because nothing was funny about the situation. The car kept going and my sister's leg was messed up. I had to help her back to school. We had a nursing room in the school, so Nicky went to see a nurse. The nurse looked at my sister's legs and found bruises on them. My sister was on crutches and couldn't attend *The Wiz* play because she could barely walk. I never thought I would see the day one of my siblings would get hit by a car.

CHAPTER 8- AGE 15

{UNNECESSARY PAIN}

We were living off Seven Mile on a street called Fenelon. There were also many memories at that house. We first moved there and were living with my cousin Lisa and her family, and my great grandmother. Me and my siblings called her the "grandma in the wheelchair" because she has always been in a wheelchair from the time we were born. Eventually, they moved out and it became our house.

My family wasn't poor, but we can say we know about the struggle. There were roaches and mice in that house. Also, the refrigerator was bad, so we had to put our food in a tote. Roaches ended up getting in there too. We had them bad, but we ended up getting rid of them. Besides that, we had a good time. Sometimes we had water flights in the house. However, with the good times comes the troubled times.

One day my mom went grocery shopping to get some food for the house. Her husband King was so controlling, and he didn't allow us to do anything. So, when we wanted to do something, we would always have to ask him. Where we were living, there was a park across the street. There were a lot of us so when we went to the park all the kids wanted to come out too. My mom's friend stayed in the projects down the street from us and they would some time come to the park. My sister, Kathy, and I were at the park with my mom's friend's daughter. My Stepdad told us to come back to the house and don't go back to the park. We were to stay on the porch.

My mom's friend's daughter came back across the street, and she was like, "Come to the park." So, we did. My Stepdad saw us and called me back across the street. He said," Didn't I tell you not to go back to the park?" Then he cut off a piece of the water hose and whooped me with it. My mom came back, but he still didn't stop. She asked what happened and told him to stop but he was the boss. He stopped when he wanted to. That day I wanted to run away to my cousin Rob's house, but I thought I couldn't leave my mom and siblings. So, I stayed. I was so angry that I just wanted to go away and never come back.

That same house is also where I met my ex-boyfriend, Matt. We went to the same school, Greenfield Park Elementary/ Middle School. His sister was in my class from the third to fifth grade. He would always drop her off to class. So, I remembered him. His brother started dating my little sister. I was scared to talk or even fall in love with a guy, so I tried to stay away from it. Eventually it got old, and I started to catch feelings for him. At some point, we had to move but didn't have anywhere to go. So, we moved into a shelter. We all were in one room, everyone except my brother, Terry.

CHAPTER 9- AGE 21

{FISH WITHOUT WATER}

After graduating High school, I soon had to try and figure out what I wanted to do. I always wanted to go to college, so that was one of my options. I just didn't know which one I wanted to attend, so I first tried Henry Ford College. Then my cousin, Beth, came up with an idea.

She knew about this college in Lansing. They had apartments, offered students a bus pass for the whole semester. They would pick you up at the apartment and drop you off by the college. So, I agreed to go, but later my cousin backed out. She explained she wasn't ready to leave, and her mom needed her. So, I ended up going by myself because I'm the type of person who likes to finish what I start.

My mom ended up moving me down to East Lansing. It was by Michigan State, so it was a party town. I had a nice apartment, but soon I would find out what it truly meant to be on your own. My mom and I got into a little debate about something small, but that caused us to not speak to each other for a couple weeks. This was when I had to really stand on my own two feet.

I had to learn how to stand up by first going to get a job. I went to Okemos Mall and filled out applications at the whole store. I was determined to get a job. My mom always said, "You're going to get some no's, but if you get one yes then that's your start." So, I was on a mission. Not only that, but I also needed food, so I had to learn how to apply for a Bridge Card. I got to see the real responsibilities of what comes first. Shoes or bills?

College was terrible too. My financial aid wasn't coming through so I couldn't get my books. I had to go to the library and write everything out. I didn't have any money, not even fifteen cents to print out a homework paper. This was supposed to be a fun experience, but I felt like my family wasn't there for me. Although my mom paid for my apartment and bought everything, I wanted them to come and visit like my roommate's family did. There was a time I got so depressed, I tried to commit suicide. I was in the tub and tried to drown myself, but instead my phone got water damaged.

Luckily my friend Justice was going to college on the west side of Lansing, so she was going through some stuff with her family as well. We were there for each other. It was a sad experience, but we made the best of it. We would listen to Gospel music anytime we felt down. We helped each other get through those rough times. Later my family came back around, but by this time I had gotten home sick. I really didn't appreciate being in Lansing. I felt like I didn't choose the right to come here, so I ended up moving back to Detroit, Michigan.

CHAPTER 10- AGE 23

{A NEW BEGINNING}

Being back in Detroit, Michigan living with family and friends made me see how much I took what I had for granted. It's true you never know the value of something until you do it yourself. Now I had time to think and make up my mind about what I really wanted to do. I wanted to start over, live a positive life without drama, and get a second chance.

This time was to be a new beginning. The first time I was trying to escape from my problems but didn't know that those problems would soon follow me knocking at my door. I wanted to do something different. I always said I wanted to build a foundation for my future. So, in order to teach others, I must start with myself.

First, I saved up enough money to move. I didn't know the life I had spoken, but I was really living it. I wanted to get close to my Father in Heaven. One day, I was talking to my mom's best friend, Francine, about the Bible. I told her I wanted to get close to Him, but I didn't know where to start because the Bible was so big. She told me to just pray about it and ask Him, and He would show me. I prayed and went to sleep not expecting to wake up the next day.

I was supposed go to DHS for an appointment that morning. Being lazy, I debated on whether I should go. I decided to go. There I was on the bus listening to my music when this lady started talking to me. I couldn't hear her because I had my headphones in, so I had to take them out. When I did, she showed me this card with Revelations, and told me her church was having a study. She helped young people get closer to their father. Immediately, I started crying. Like were you there? How do you know I was just praying about this last night?

From there we exchanged numbers. It was her and another lady that would meet with me on Thursdays to have Bible study in the Lansing College Library. I started attending church and going over to the woman's house for dinner. We had some nice times. The church would have church outings. At one of the outings, this man at the church asked me, "Are you ready?"

I said to him, "Ready for what?"

He said, "This journey because the Lord is about to take you places you have never been."

He didn't lie because from there on I was a social butterfly. I was everywhere. Even my roommates were getting jealous because this second time around I knew what I had worked hard for, and I wasn't going to let anything stop me from enjoying life. This was my second chance to appreciate what I had. I met all types of diverse people from all over the world. It was interesting to know there were other people who were doing what I was. I thought I was the only person lost. This experience really opened my eyes and took me out of my comfort zone.

I started talking to random people. I know they were looking like who is this girl? I was thinking the same, but I knew it was something greater that was leading me to speak to them. Ordinarily, I would be too shy and scared to even approach a stranger. I had talks with a bus driver and a lawyer in the bathroom. They were explaining to me their story of where they came from. This made me see that everyone has a story, and you never know what a person has been through unless they tell you. I was honored to be able to speak to them about their story and share my journey too.

The women at the church were very sweet and kind. I learned a lot from them. Since I was dating this guy named Drew, in one of our studies they told me, "Make sure the person you're dating is on the same page as you or they will bring you down." I thought, well he goes to church so he should be straight. I really didn't understand exactly what they were saying. This was what caused me to move back with his family. Being stupid in love caused me to lose everything.

CHAPTER 11-AGE 24-25

{LEARNING EXPERIENCE}

Once I was back in Detroit again, Drew's mom offered me a place to stay at her house since my family and I wasn't on good terms. It's true when they say you never know a person until you live with them. Drew and I had broken up at this time.

This was because before I had to move back, Drew's brother had invited me to come to a Halloween party. However, Drew wanted me to stay at my apartment, but I had told my niece and nephew I was going to get them. This was our yearly ritual. I would buy their costumes, and we would go trick or treating. So, I was taking them. He didn't like it, so he was like fine I'll get somebody else to go with me. That was it. I got there, and I saw why he didn't want me at the Halloween party.

Living with Drew and his family was a learning experience. This man was very disrespectful. Although we weren't together, I did consider him a friend. He would lie to his girlfriends and say things like; I was his cousin's ex, I was nobody, or I'm only there because I do so much for the family and his stepdad wanted to pay me back by letting me stay there. He told his friends I begged him to go with me. He lied because I wasn't even interested in him honestly. Being raised on the east side, I was always attracted to bad boys. He was soft as a cotton ball. What attracted me to him was because of our conversations, I thought he was a nice person.

Being in the house, I saw exactly what he was doing to me behind closed doors. Lying to these females. One would call and he would say, "I'm at the gym," but be sitting on the couch with another female. Wanting to find a way out, I didn't know I would soon get back in touch with Paul years later.

My sister had already started back talking to the brother, Carl. However, I wasn't looking to be in a relationship, especially after what happened to me with my ex-boyfriend, Drew. For me, going down to visit Paul was more of a way of escape. My sister and I would go down every weekend to visit, taking turns driving back in forth.

We fell in love with Carl and Paul's mom, Patty. She offered me the chance to come stay with her, but after living with people, I just didn't want to live with anybody else. People often say they're going to help you but use you. Not her though. Patty was sweet. This woman, even to this day has done so much for me, and my siblings and included the family. She's the type of woman who would miss sleep just to make sure you're okay and go the extra mile for anyone.

When I lived with her, she didn't charge me for anything, not even gas money. She let me use her car anytime I had to work. Even when I finally got my own house, she was the one who came and helped me paint my kitchen and throw my housewarming/ birthday party at my new place. She's really my second mom for sure.

CHAPTER 12- AGE 27

{AWAKENING}

My first tattoo June 16, 2013

"With everything I had been through or experienced I just wished I had wings to fly away."

After experiencing so much, I just knew there had to be a way I could escape all the negative things that were happening in my life. I was just sitting in my room at Nicky's house, thinking of ways to escape. I then picked up my phone and started watching YouTube. As I was scrolling through my phone to see what to watch, I clicked on this guy named Aaron Doughty.

He had some videos on there. I clicked on the one that said meditations. He said, "Listen to this for thirty days and I guarantee it will change your life." Not really listening to that, I clicked on it, I just wanted to feel free from everything. So, I listened to it in the morning and at night for a whole month. Wow, after listening to it I realized this man didn't lie.

One day I was meditating and as I was relaxing and listening to his voice. I didn't know

I was going to see a little girl. It showed me that she was scared and wanted to be free. The reason I have a love for kids is because of her. Once she gets around kids that's when she's most vulnerable in herself. As I experienced this, I'm crying because this little girl was me as a kid being molested. I thought I let it go and I was over it, but this showed me I was still holding on to the past. I had to release her to be free. In this meditation, I understood how it was me who chose Jackson, and me who really reached out to Paul. So, it wasn't him. It was really me. This gave me my power back once I woke up to my truth. I continued to watch Aaron Doughty every day.

I was struggling trying to figure out what business I wanted to open. I never thought about recreation although I was working for one at the time. So, on one of his videos, he asked what are you passionate about? Instantly after hearing that a light bulb came on. I thought to myself about how as a kid I always said every child born is the future. That's how I envision my brand, *Kids Are The Future*, (K.A.T.F). Whatever legacy you leave behind is what your kids will live on and pass on to their kids. It just continues to repeat years and years to come.

Now, leaving a legacy is what I live for every day. I don't want to just exist. I want to offer, contribute, and distribute my gift to the world. We all have a little girl and boy who is waiting for us to release them and grow through the process. I finally answered the call. Will you?

WHEN SHE CRIES

by

Author Cornelious Woody Sr.

She cries sometimes when the wind blows
heavily preventing the birds from reaching the
skies~ She cries when day has no beginning of
meaning and night has no ending pending
beautifully~ She cries beneath sunglasses to
disguise the sorrow of the day and tomorrow that
never seems to go away~ She cries because
everything he had been taken~ warped her mind
body and soul everything unfolds and
heartbreaking~ She cries watching her family

tree slowly dies before her watered eyes~ She cries for love, cries for hugs, cries for destiny to fulfill happiness within wounded doves~
She cries a million tears no one ever seems to hear~ mourning so clear while selfishness extremely bold and sincere~ She cries when there is no sunshine or sunrise her emotions tied and paralyzed~ Cries when not a single red rose of love makes it out the lonely garden alive~ She cries~ She cries~ She cries.

Made in the USA
Middletown, DE
27 June 2023

33971712R00050